KIDS COOK MICROWAVE

A RECIPE BOOK FOR CHILDREN

DELICIOUS, NUTRITIOUS AND FUN FOODS TO COOK IN THE MICROWAVE

This book belongs to:

_____

Given to me by:

_____

HPBooks®

D1557721

Published by HPBooks ®, P.O. Box 5367, Tucson, AZ 85703
602/888-2150
ISBN 0-89586-271-9
Library of Congress Catalog Card No. 83-81139
Designed by Ron Emal.
Printed in U.S.A.

TO MOM:

There are some important rules of microwave cooking that assure your child a successful product. Remember that there are many similarities between microwave and conventional cooking. Microwave cooking will become as easy as conventional cooking with some practice. The fun is in the practicing!

In this book we have decided to use percentage of powers instead of using the names of the power levels. If there are any questions, your owner's manual should convert power levels to percentages.

REMEMBER

In microwave cooking, the temperature of the food determines the time of cooking. The colder the food, the longer it takes to cook. The volume, amount and size or thickness of the food will also affect the time of cooking. The more food you have, the longer it will take to cook. For example, one medium-size potato will take 4-1/2 minutes and four medium-size potatoes will take 18 to 20 minutes.

With your patience, microwave cooking will be fun and rewarding for your child!

Happy Microwaving

Janet
and
Barbara

Table of Contents

BEGINNINGS

"Important points you need
to know before you start!"

* Microwave Safety

* How To Use A Recipe

* Food Groups

* Microwave Cooking Terms

* Utensils

* This = That

* Table Arrangements

* Kid's Table Style

SAFETY

"Microwave Cooking is really fun,
especially when we follow Safety Rules."

REMEMBER ALWAYS

* Use pot holders

* Never run the microwave empty

* Use microwave-safe dishes, such as glass
  or paper

* DO NOT USE METAL

* Don't pop popcorn in a brown-paper bag

* Never cook an egg in its shell

* Follow mother's Safety Rules

HOW TO USE A RECIPE

INGREDIENTS:

A clean kitchen and a clean you.

All utensils and ingredients organized in one area.

DIRECTIONS:

Read the recipe completely, making sure you understand all the steps.

Measure everything carefully. Follow all microwave instructions and pay close attention to cooking TIME & VARIABLE COOKING POWERS.

Be sure to clean up everything so that mom will enjoy your working in the kitchen.

FOOD GROUPS

When planning meals, consider the "Basic 4" food groups. No one food contains all the nutrients we need in the amounts we need. We must choose from a variety of foods contained in the "Basic 4" food groups.

1. Fruits & Vegetables
(4 or more servings per day)

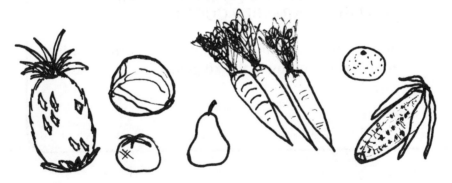

2. Breads & Cereals
(4 servings per day)

3. Meat, Fish, Poultry
(2 servings per day)

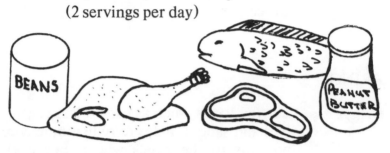

4. Dairy Products
(3 servings per day)

MICROWAVE COOKING TERMS

ARRANGING FOODS

> It is important to place more dense, thick foods near the outer edge of the dish. Porous, small foods should be placed near the center.

STIRRING

> Stirring foods, such as casseroles, vegetables and sauces, helps to redistribute cool portions to the edges where they cook faster.

TURNING

> Large foods, such as roasts and poultry, are turned over during cooking to allow for even penetration of microwave energy from all sides.

PIERCE

Food that has a protective skin or membrane covering should be pierced with a fork; this allows steam and pressure to escape. If food is not pierced, it will explode. Examples are egg yolks and whites, potatoes and whole squash.

BROWNING AIDS

Since there is less browning with microwave cooking, better browning is achieved with browning aids. Aids include bottled brown bouquet sauce, dry soup or gravy mixes, crumb coatings and paprika.

STANDING TIME

Let food stand a few minutes before serving. This allows heat at the outside of the food to penetrate to the center without continued cooking on the outside.

UTENSILS

Liquid Measuring Cup
See-through glass

Dry Measuring Cups
Graduated: 1/4, 1/3, 1/2, 1 cup

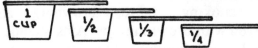

Custard Cup

Cutting Board

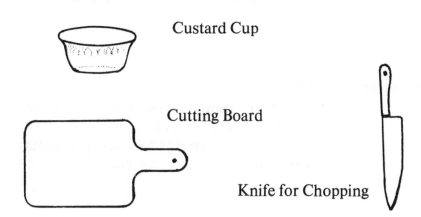

Knife for Chopping

 Mixing Bowls

 Electric Mixer

 Vegetable Peeler

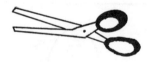 Vegetable Shears

 Measuring Spoons
1/4 tsp., 1/2 tsp., 1 tsp., 1 tbsp.

THIS = THAT

3 teaspoons = ———— 1 tablespoon

4 tablespoons = ———— 1/4 cup

8 tablespoons = ———— 1/2 cup

16 tablespoons = ———— 1 cup

2 cups = ———— 1 pint

2 pints = ———— 1 quart

2 quarts = ———— 1/2 gallon

THIS = THAT

APPLES
    1 pound   3 medium (3 cups sliced)

BREAD
    1 pound loaf   14 to 20 slices

BUTTER
    1 stick   8 tablespoons or 1/2 cup

CHEDDAR CHEESE
    1/4 pound   1 cup shredded

FLOUR, ALL-PURPOSE
    1 pound   4 cups

MACARONI
    1 cup uncooked   2 to 2-1/4 cups cooked
    1/2 pound uncooked   4 cups cooked

NOODLES
    1 cup uncooked   1-3/4 cups cooked
    1/2 pound uncooked   4 to 5 cups cooked

ONION
    1 small   1/4 cup chopped
    1 medium   1/2 cup chopped
    1 large   1 cup

WHITE POTATOES
    1 pound   3 medium
                             2 cups mashed
                             2-1/3 to 2-1/2 cups sliced

REGULAR RICE
    1 pound   2-1/2 cups uncooked
                           8 cups cooked

TABLE ARRANGEMENTS

Mealtime can be more interesting with an attractive table setting. Variations may be made depending on the menu and the family needs.

* A tablecloth or placemat can make the meal more attractive.

* A centerpiece is nice—perhaps a fresh or artificial flower.

* Omit any eating utensils if not needed during the meal.

* If only a spoon and fork are needed, place them to the right of the plate.

* Spoons and forks are placed with the piece to be used first on the outside.

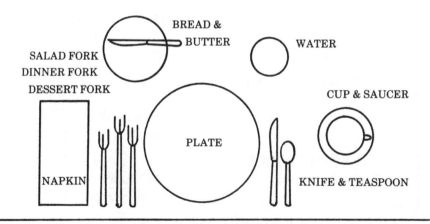

KID'S TABLE STYLE

Wear a smile when you come to the table and try to make each meal a pleasant meal. Good table manners at home builds self-confidence away from home.

A FEW TIPS TO HELP OUT:

* Chew food with mouth closed.

* Keep table talk pleasant and interesting to the family or friends.

* Ask for what you want instead of reaching for it.

* Say "PLEASE" and "THANK YOU."

* After silverware is used, place it on the plate.

* Foods such as breads, crackers, cookies, olives, pickles and nuts may be eaten with your fingers.

* Try a little of all foods and be positive.

* The napkin may be partly folded and placed to the left of the plate.

* Be excused when finished eating.

BREAKFAST

Growing boys and girls need to start their day with a wonderful wake-up. The microwave will help you begin everyday deliciously. For a fast bite on the run before school or activities, the following recipes are sure to please. GOOD MORNING!

"Start your day the right way with a quick nutritious microwave breakfast."

BREAKFAST

THIS MORNING'S SPECIAL

EGGS

Eggs should never be microwaved in their shells. Pressure will build up within the egg, causing it to explode. Eggs cook quickly and continue to cook after microwave power is off. Cook eggs until they appear moist. They will be tough and rubbery if overcooked.

SCRAMBLED EGG

- 1 egg
- 1 tablespoon water or milk

In a 1-cup glass measure or coffee cup, stir together egg and water or milk. Cook on HIGH power 40 to 45 seconds or on 50% power 1-1/2 minutes. Scrambled eggs come out light and fluffy.
Serves 1.

POACHED EGG

- 1/4 cup water
- 1 egg

Microwave water in custard cup or coffee cup 1 minute on HIGH power. Add egg; puncture yolk with a fork. Cover with plastic wrap and cook 35 seconds on HIGH power.
Serves 1.

BAKED EGG

- 1/4 teaspoon butter or margarine
- 1 egg

Place butter or margarine in custard cup. Cook 15 seconds to melt butter or margarine. Add egg; puncture yolk with fork. Cover with plastic wrap and cook 1 minute 12 seconds on 50% power or until white is set.
Serves 1.

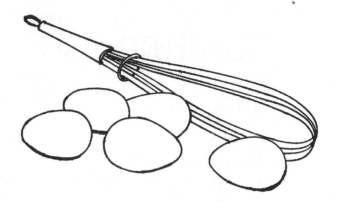

ARIZONA EGGS

- 8 eggs
- 1/2 cup milk
- 1 (4-oz.) can chopped green chilies
- 1/3 cup chopped green onions
- 1-1/2 cups shredded Cheddar cheese

Beat eggs well. Add milk, green chilies, green onions and cheese. Microwave 8 to 9 minutes on 60% power, stirring several times. Eggs will be done when they still look moist. Let stand 1 minute, then serve eggs warm.

Serves 4.

BREAKFAST MEATS

— BACON —

Bacon can be microwaved on a bacon rack, between sheets of paper towels, or on paper plates or everyday plates.

The rule of thumb with bacon is: 1 minute per slice up to six slices. Additional slices are 30 seconds per slice on HIGH power.

1 slice bacon	1 minute
2 slices bacon	2 minutes
3 slices bacon	3 minutes
4 slices bacon	4 minutes
5 slices bacon	5 minutes
6 slices bacon	6 minutes
7 slices bacon	6-1/2 minutes
8 slices bacon	7 minutes
9 slices bacon	7-1/2 minutes
10 slices bacon	8 minutes
11 slices bacon	8-1/2 minutes
12 slices bacon	9 minutes

```
* * HOT TIP * *

Grease gets hot in the microwave! So
beware when cooking foods like bacon
or sausage. Even the grease on the paper
towel can burn you.
```

HAM SLICES

Place 1/4-inch ham slices on plate. Cover with
waxed paper. Cook in microwave on HIGH power.

Ham slices should be about the same size and shape.
If not, place small slices to the center.

1 slice — 1 to 1-1/2 minutes
2 slices — 2 to 2-1/2 minutes
3 slices — 3 to 3-1/2 minutes
4 slices — 4 to 4-1/2 minutes

⊂⊃⊂⊃ SAUSAGE ⊂⊃⊂⊃

- 2 sausage links or preformed patties

Place 2 sausage links or patties on a microwave rack or dish. Brush with a browning agent for eye appeal. Cover with a paper towel. Cook 1 to 1-1/2 minutes on HIGH power.

Breakfast sausage cooks quickly and doesn't brown. It will be more attractive if brushed with a browning agent before cooking. Use equal parts of browning agent and water. It is nice to keep this mixture on hand for other meat products.

FRENCH TOAST

- 1 egg
- 1 slice bread

Beat 1 egg in a cereal bowl. Dip 1 slice of bread in egg, turning until well coated. Place bread on plate. Pour remaining egg on top. Cook 1 minute on HIGH power. Top with butter, syrup or your favorite jam.
Serves 1.

COOKED CEREAL

OATMEAL

- 1/3 cup quick-cooking oatmeal
- 3/4 cup water
- 1/8 teaspoon salt

In a large bowl, combine all ingredients. Cook 1-1/2 to 2-1/2 minutes on HIGH power, stirring several times. Top with raisins or nuts. Allow to stand 3 minutes.
Serves 1.

CREAM OF WHEAT

- 2-1/2 tablespoons Cream of Wheat
- 1 cup water
- 1/8 teaspoon salt

In a large bowl, combine Cream of Wheat, water and salt. Cook 3 to 4 minutes on HIGH power, stirring often. Allow to stand 2 to 3 minutes.
Serves 1.

BREAKFAST RING

- 1/3 cup butter or margarine
- 1/3 cup brown sugar
- 1 tablespoon water
- 1 teaspoon cinnamon
- 3 to 4 tablespoons raisins
- 1/3 cup chopped nuts
- 1 (8-oz.) can refrigerated biscuits

In a round 8-inch glass dish, combine butter or margarine, brown sugar, water and cinnamon. Microwave 35 to 45 seconds on HIGH power or until butter or margarine is melted. Stir in raisins and nuts. Cut each biscuit in 4 pieces. Add to other ingredients. Mix carefully with a fork until all biscuits are coated. Push biscuits away from center. Place custard cup in center forming a ring. Cook uncovered 4 minutes on HIGH power. Turn ring onto serving platter.

Serves 5 to 6.

PEANUT-BUTTER MUFFINS

- 3/4 cup milk
- 1/4 cup sugar
- 1 egg
- 1/4 cup peanut butter
- 2 tablespoons salad oil
- 2 cups biscuit mix

Combine milk, sugar, egg, peanut butter and oil in a medium-size bowl. Blend well. Add biscuit mix to milk mixture; stir well until flour is moistened.

Line microwave muffin maker with paper muffin cups. Fill paper cups half full.

Place 6 muffins in microwave oven. Microwave uncovered on HIGH power 2 to 4 minutes or until toothpick inserted in center comes out clean. Cook remaining 6 muffins.

Top with 1/2 teaspoon of your favorite jam or jelly.

Makes 12 muffins.

HOT CHOCOLATE

- 1/4 cup unsweetened cocoa
- 1/4 cup sugar
- 1 teaspoon cinnamon
- 3 cups milk

Combine cocoa, sugar and cinnamon in 2-quart glass measure. Add milk; stir well. Microwave 3 to 4 minutes on HIGH power; stir and microwave another 3 to 4 minutes on 60% power or until steaming hot. Be careful that the milk doesn't boil. If you use the probe, take the temperature to 140F.

Serves 2 to 3.

NOTES

LUNCH

To stay full of pep, be sure to include lunch in your everyday plans. Eating a little of every kind of food served at lunch will help you grow and keep your body in good repair. A good variety of meats, fruits and vegetables, dairy foods and cereal foods will give you energy and sparkle for the rest of the day.

LUNCH

"Treats For You And A Friend"

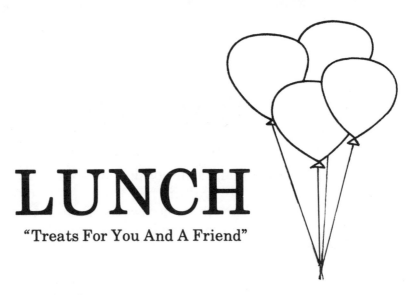

HOT DOGS

Place hot dog in a split hot-dog bun. Wrap loosely in paper towel to prevent the bun from becoming soggy. Place hot dog in the microwave. Follow the chart below for the plain hot dog or any of the other hot-dog recipes.

1 hot dog	30 to 45 seconds
2 hot dogs	45 to 50 seconds
3 hot dogs	1 to 1-1/2 minutes
4 hot dogs	1-1/2 to 2 minutes
5 hot dogs	2 to 2-1/2 minutes

Defrost hot dog first if frozen.

CHEESY HOT DOG

Slash hot dog lengthwise, but not completely through. Place in bun. Fill hot-dog center with 1/4-inch slice of cheese. Microwave on HIGH power on paper plate or towel 30 to 45 seconds.
Serves 1.

PIZZA DOG

Slash hot dog lengthwise, but not completely through. Place in bun. Spread center of hot dog with pizza sauce, ketchup or tomato sauce. Sprinkle with Italian seasoning and mozzarella cheese. Microwave on HIGH power on paper plate or towel 30 to 45 seconds.

Serves 1.

HOT DOG ON A STICK

Insert wooden ice-cream stick in hot dog lengthwise 1-1/2 to 2 inches. Microwave on paper plate 30 to 45 seconds on HIGH power. Serve with mustard, ketchup or relish.

Serves 1.

CONEY ISLAND DOGS

- 1 (15-oz.) can chili with beans
- 1 package hot dogs
- 8 hot-dog buns, split
- 1/2 cup grated cheese

Place chili in glass bowl. Microwave 2 minutes on HIGH power. Stir. Microwave another minute or until hot and bubbly. Set aside. Place hot dogs on open buns on a paper plate. Microwave 1-1/2 to 2 minutes or until warm. Spoon chili over hot dogs. Sprinkle cheese on top.

Serves 5 to 6.

SANDWICHES

Hot microwaved sandwiches are delicious and heat very quickly. Be careful not to overcook. Heat bread on 50% power until warm and not hot. Day-old bread or toasted breads are excellent to microwave because they are drier. Fresh bread has a lot of moisture that can sometimes cause the bread to be soggy. For heating sandwiches, wrap them individually in paper towels which will absorb the moisture. Mustard, mayonnaise, pickles or other topping should be added after the sandwich is heated. Several thin slices of meat heat better than one thick slice. Because meat and fillings are dense and bread is porous, the fillings absorb more energy and become hotter than the bread. Be careful and allow sandwiches to stand a few minutes before eating or the filling may burn your mouth.

TOASTED CHEESE

Toast 2 slices bread in conventional toaster. When toasted, place 1 slice of your favorite cheese between the toasted bread. Place sandwich in microwave. Cook 1 minute on 70% power.

Be careful! Cheese melts quickly in the microwave and becomes tough and rubbery when overcooked.

TUNA-PIZZA BURGER

- 1 (6-1/2-oz.) can tuna
- 1/4 cup diced celery
- 3 tablespoons mayonnaise
- 4 slices toast or 2 English muffins, cut in half
- 1 (10-oz.) can pizza sauce
- Grated Parmesan cheese

Mix together tuna, celery and mayonnaise. Pile tuna mixture on toasted bread or muffins. Spoon pizza sauce on top. Sprinkle with Parmesan cheese. Place pizza burgers on a plate. Microwave 1-1/2 to 2 minutes on 70% power.

Serves 4.

SLOPPY JOES

- 1 pound ground beef
- 1/2 cup chopped onions
- 1/2 cup chopped green pepper
- 1/2 teaspoon paprika
- 1 (8-oz.) can tomato sauce
- 2 tablespoons brown sugar
- 1 teaspoon salt
- 4 toasted hamburger buns

Combine ground beef, onions and green pepper.

Microwave 4 to 5 minutes on HIGH power or until meat is no longer pink. Crumble with fork; add paprika, tomato sauce, brown sugar and salt. Blend well. Cook covered on 60% power 7 minutes, stirring once. Spoon onto buns.

Serves 4.

SUPER HEROES

- 1 small loaf French or Italian bread
- 2 slices salami
- 2 slices ham
- 2 slices bologna
- 1 large tomato, sliced
- 2 slices American cheese
- 2 slices Swiss cheese
- Lettuce
- Dill or sweet pickles
- Mayonnaise or butter

Cut bread in half; then cut each half the long way.

On one side of each half loaf, select one or all of your favorite fillers—salami, ham, bologna, lettuce, tomato slices, pickles and cheese. Spread mayonnaise or butter on the other half and place on top. Wrap each sandwich in paper towel. Microwave 1-1/2 minutes on 50% power.

Makes 2 sandwiches.

PEANUT-BUTTER SANDWICHES

Everyone's favorite sandwich filling forms the base for hot and fresh sandwiches you can microwave yourself.

- 1 slice toast
- 1-1/2 tablespoons peanut butter

Spread peanut butter on toast. Top with your choice of jelly, marshmallows, banana slices or grated cheese. Place sandwich on napkin. Microwave 15 to 20 seconds on HIGH power or until melted.
Serves 1.

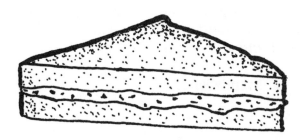

SOUPS

Your favorite canned soup heats quickly in the microwave. In a 4-cup glass measure, combine soup and 1 can of water or milk depending on the soup you choose. Microwave 2 to 3 minutes on HIGH power, or insert probe and microwave to 130F. Stir after 2 minutes.

QUICK CHILI

- 1/2 cup chopped onion
- 1 pound ground beef
- 1 (16-oz.) can tomatoes
- 1 (16-oz.) can kidney beans, drained
- 1 teaspoon salt
- 1 teaspoon chili powder

In a plastic collander, combine onion and ground beef. Place collander in a glass pie plate to catch grease. Microwave 4 to 5 minutes on HIGH power. Carefully place ground-beef mixture in serving container. Add tomatoes, kidney beans, salt and chili powder. Microwave 10 to 12 minutes at 70% power, stirring several times.
Serves 4 to 5.

TACOS

- 1 pound ground beef
- 1 (8-oz.) can tomato sauce
- 1 package taco-seasoning mix
- 6 taco shells

Microwave ground beef 4 to 5 minutes on HIGH power or until no longer pink. Drain. Add tomato sauce and taco-seasoning mix. Microwave 3 to 5 minutes. Stir well. Serve in taco shells.

Makes 5 to 6 tacos.

BEAN BURROS

- 1/2 cup chopped onion
- 1/4 cup chopped green pepper
- 1 to 2 cups leftover roast beef
- 1 (4-oz.) can diced green chilies
- 1 (16-oz.) can refried beans
- 6 (12-inch) flour tortillas
- 1 cup grated Cheddar cheese

Microwave onion and green pepper 1 to 2 minutes on HIGH power. Cut beef into small pieces. Add chilies and beans. Microwave 3 to 4 minutes on HIGH power. Place 1/4 cup bean mixture on each tortilla; fold in half. Top with cheese. Microwave 6 burros 2-1/2 minutes on 70% power or until cheese is melted. One burro will take 45 seconds on HIGH power.

Serves 6.

CHEESE CRISP

On a paper plate, microwave one 10- to 12-inch flour tortilla 2 minutes or until crisp. Turn tortilla over and cover with grated cheese. Microwave 1 minute on HIGH power or 2 minutes on 50% power until cheese melts.

Serves 3 to 4.

DINNER

The aim of this chapter is to provide nutritious, delicious and easy meals that everyone loves.

Vegetables will be fresh or frozen and attractively served. Vegetables are always cooked on HIGH power and cooked covered.

Casseroles can be cooked by time or a temperature probe. If you want to use the probe, insert it into the center of the casserole and cook to 150F.

Your family will be very pleased with your dinner results.

DINNER

MAIN COURSE

EXTRAS

MEATY MACARONI

- 1 pound ground beef
- 1 (15-oz.) can tomato sauce
- 1-1/2 cups elbow macaroni, uncooked
- 1 cup water
- 1/2 teaspoon Italian seasoning
- 1 cup shredded Cheddar cheese

Cook ground beef 4 to 5 minutes on HIGH power in a plastic collander placed in a dish to catch the grease. In a large casserole, combine ground beef, tomato sauce, uncooked macaroni, water and Italian seasoning. Cook on HIGH power, covered, 12 to 14 minutes. Stir halfway through cooking time. Sprinkle cheese on top. Let stand covered 4 to 6 minutes before serving.
Serves 4.

MACARONI
AND CHEESE
WITH FRANKS

- 1 cup elbow macaroni, uncooked
- 1 cup water
- 1/2 cup milk
- 1 tablespoon all-purpose flour
- 1/2 teaspoon dry mustard
- 1/4 cup chopped green pepper
- 4 frankfurters, cut into 1-inch pieces
- 1-1/2 cups grated Cheddar cheese

Place macaroni and water in a 2-quart casserole. Cover and microwave 4 to 5 minutes on HIGH power or until boiling. Let stand 5 minutes. Stir in milk, flour, mustard and green pepper. Add frankfurters and cheese. Cover tightly and microwave on HIGH power 4 minutes or until cheese is melted.

Serves 4.

WIENER CASSEROLE

- 1 (10-oz.) package frozen French-style green beans
- 1/4 cup sliced green onions
- 1 (10-oz.) can cream of chicken soup
- 1/2 cup milk
- 1/2 cup grated Cheddar cheese
- 5 to 6 wieners, cut in 1-inch pieces

In a covered casserole, microwave green beans and onions 6 to 7 minutes on HIGH power. In a 4-cup glass measure, combine soup, milk and cheese. Microwave 2 to 3 minutes or until cheese is melted. Stir after 2 minutes. Add wieners, green beans and onions. Microwave 3 minutes or until hot.

Serves 6.

TUNA-CHIPS CASSEROLE

- 2 (6-1/2-oz.) cans tuna, drained
- 1 (10-3/4-oz.) can cream of mushroom or celery soup
- 1/2 cup milk
- 1 tablespoon Worcestershire sauce
- 1/2 cup grated Cheddar cheese
- 1 cup crushed potato chips

Mix drained tuna with undiluted soup, milk and Worcestershire sauce. Turn into a 1-1/2-quart casserole. Microwave 4 to 5 minutes on HIGH power. Sprinkle cheese and potato chips on top of hot casserole.

Serves 4.

MEXICAN CHICKEN

- 2 cups small corn chips
- 2 cups cooked chicken or turkey, cut in cubes
- 1 (10-oz.) can cream of chicken soup
- 1 (4-oz.) can diced green chilies
- 2 medium tomatoes, cut up
- 1 cup grated Cheddar cheese
- 1 cup dairy sour cream

Arrange corn chips in the bottom of a glass casserole. Scatter chicken or turkey pieces on top of chips. Mix soup and chilies together in medium bowl; pour over chicken mixture. Place tomatoes on top and sprinkle on grated cheese. Microwave 12 to 15 minutes on 50% power. Garnish with sour cream.
Serves 4.

TACO CHICKEN

- 1 pound chicken pieces—pick your favorite
- 1 beaten egg
- 1 cup crushed cheesy crackers
- 2 tablespoons taco-seasoning mix

Combine crackers and taco-seasoning mix; set aside. Dip chicken pieces in egg; then roll in cracker mixture. Place chicken pieces in a round glass dish with thicker pieces to the outside. Microwave on HIGH power 7 to 8 minutes.

Serves 4.

QUICK TAMALE PIE

- 1 (15-oz.) can chili
- 1 (12-oz.) can whole-kernel corn, drained
- 1 cup grated Cheddar cheese
- 1 to 1-1/2 cups crumbled corn chips

Layer bottom of a 2-quart casserole with chili. Top with corn and cheese. Sprinkle corn chips over top. Microwave 5 minutes on HIGH power.
Serves 4.

GOLDEN NUGGETS

- 1 pound ground beef or ground turkey
- 1/4 cup chopped onion
- 1 egg
- 1/2 cup dry breadcrumbs
- 1 teaspoon fennel or Italian seasoning
- 1/2 teaspoon salt
- 1/2 pound Cheddar cheese, cut into 1/2-inch cubes
- 1 (10-3/4-oz.) can tomato soup
- Grated cheese

Mix all ingredients except cheeses and soup. Form a meatball around each cheese cube. Microwave meatballs 5 to 6 minutes on HIGH power or until done. Top with tomato soup. Cover and microwave another 3 to 4 minutes on HIGH power. Top with grated cheese.

Serves 4 to 5.

BAKED POTATOES

Choose a medium-size baking potato for each person. Wash and scrub the skin of each potato. Dry with paper towels. Puncture each potato twice with a fork. Place potatoes on a paper towel in microwave oven, 1-inch apart. Turn potatoes over and rearrange after half of cooking time.

MICROWAVE ON HIGH POWER

1 potato —————————— 4 to 6 minutes

2 potatoes —————————— 6 to 8 minutes

3 potatoes —————————— 8 to 12 minutes

4 potatoes —————————— 12 to 16 minutes

5 potatoes —————————— 16 to 20 minutes

Let stand a few minutes. Cut an "X" in each potato. Insert a square of butter or margarine. Serve right away.

SCALLOPED POTATOES

- 3 tablespoons butter or margarine
- 3 tablespoons all-purpose flour
- 1/2 teaspoon dry mustard
- 1 teaspoon salt
- 1-1/2 cups milk
- 4 to 5 medium potatoes, peeled, sliced
- Grated cheese
- Paprika

Microwave butter or margarine in a 4-cup glass measure 40 seconds on HIGH power. Add flour, mustard and salt. Blend well. Add milk. Microwave 4 minutes on HIGH power stirring after 2 minutes. Layer potatoes and sauce in casserole. Cover and microwave 10 to 15 minutes or until potatoes are tender. Top with grated cheese and paprika.

Serves 5 to 6.

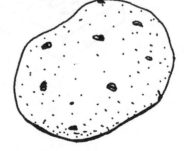

FROZEN VEGETABLES

- 1 (10-oz.) box frozen vegetables

Place box of vegetables in serving dish. Microwave on HIGH power 6 to 7 minutes. Open box and place vegetables in serving dish. Season with butter or margarine, salt and pepper.

Serves 3 to 4.

WHOLE CAULIFLOWER

Wash and trim leaves from cauliflower. Place cauliflower on serving plate. Cover with plastic wrap. Microwave 5 to 7 minutes or until tender. Top with grated cheese.
Serves 4.

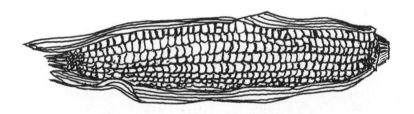

CORN ON THE COB

Clean 1 ear of corn for each person. Wrap in waxed paper, twisting the ends. Microwave 2 minutes per ear of corn on HIGH power. Serve with butter or margarine, salt and pepper.

BUTTERED CARROTS

- 2 cups carrots, sliced 1/4 inch thick
- 2 tablespoons butter or margarine

Microwave in covered casserole 5 to 6 minutes or until tender on HIGH power. Season with your favorite spice or a little parsley.
Serves 3 to 4.

YUMMY ZUCCHINI

- 3 medium zucchini

Cut zucchini into 1/2-inch pieces. Place zucchini in covered casserole. Microwave on HIGH power 6 to 7 minutes. Season with butter or margarine, salt and pepper.
Serves 5 to 6.

RICE
A LA MICROWAVE

- 2 cups hot tap water
- 1 cup rice, uncooked
- 1 teaspoon salt
- 1 teaspoon butter or margarine

Place all ingredients in 1-1/2-quart casserole. Microwave on HIGH power 5 minutes. Cover and let stand 10 minutes. Microwave on HIGH power again 5 minutes.

Serves 4.

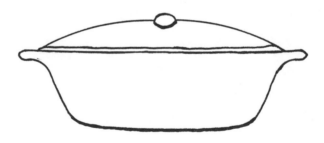

SNACKS

The microwave oven really makes snacks and desserts a treat.

Arrange small pieces of snacks in a circle so they heat more evenly.

Use waxed paper to loosely cover most snacks to hold in heat and prevent splattering.

Most snacks and desserts can be made ahead of time and stored in air-tight containers, the refrigerator or freezer.

SNACKS

"SPECIAL TREATS"

APPLESAUCE

- 6 cups apples (about 7 apples), peeled,
    cut in small pieces
- 1/2 cup sugar
- 1 teaspoon cinnamon

Combine apples, sugar and cinnamon. Microwave 6 to 7 minutes on HIGH power or until apples are tender.

Time will vary with variety of apples used and with size of apple pieces.

Use Gravenstein or McIntosh apples for the best results. You may need to add a little water if sauce looks too thick after cooking.

Serves 5 to 6.

CRISPY APPLE CRUNCH

- 4 medium apples, sliced
- 1/2 cup butter or margarine
- 3/4 cup brown sugar
- 3/4 cup quick-cooking oats
- 1/2 cup all-purpose flour
- 1 teaspoon cinnamon
- 1/2 teaspoon allspice

Spread apples evenly in an 8-inch square glass dish. Place butter or margarine in small glass mixing bowl. Microwave on 30% power 45 seconds to 1 minute until softened. Add brown sugar, cooking oats, flour, cinnamon and allspice. Mix until crumbly. Sprinkle mixture over apples.

Microwave on HIGH power 8 to 10 minutes or until apples are tender. Top with ice cream, if desired.

Serves 3 to 4.

CHOCOLATE SPIDERS

- 1 (8-oz.) milk-chocolate bar
- 2 cups crisp rice cereal
- 1/2 cup shredded coconut

Melt chocolate bar 1 to 2 minutes on 50% power. Stir in rice cereal and coconut. Drop from teaspoon onto waxed paper. Refrigerate until set.
Makes 2 dozen.

PEANUT-CHOCOLATE HAYSTACKS

- 1 (6-oz.) package semisweet chocolate pieces
- 1/2 cup chunky peanut butter
- 1 (3-oz.) can chow mein noodles

In a 2-quart glass measure or large bowl, melt chocolate pieces and peanut butter on 50% power 4 to 5 minutes. Stir after 2 minutes. Add noodles; toss well with fork.
Drop 1-1/2-inch clusters of haystacks onto waxed paper. Cool.
Makes 3 dozen.

BUTTERSCOTCH KRUNCHIES

"Quick and easy—a good source of nutrition!"

- 1 (12-oz.) package butterscotch or chocolate pieces
- 1 cup crunchy peanut butter
- 1 cup quick-cooking oats
- 1 cup whole-grain-cereal flakes
- 1 cup raisins
- 1 cup coconut, if desired

Melt butterscotch or chocolate pieces on 50% power 4 to 5 minutes in a large bowl. Stir in peanut butter, oats, cereal, raisins and coconut. Spread mixture in a buttered 11" x 7" pan. Chill and cut into squares.
Makes 35 squares.

S'MORES

- 2 graham cracker squares
- 1/2 of a plain chocolate candy bar
- 1 large marshmallow

For each serving, place 4 squares of a chocolate bar and 1 marshmallow on a graham cracker. Microwave on HIGH power 15 to 20 seconds or until marshmallow puffs. Top with second graham cracker. Eat S'mores like a sandwich.

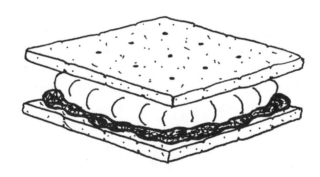

MARSHMALLOW CRISPY BARS

- 1/4 cup butter or margarine
- 30 large marshmallows
- 5 cups crisp rice cereal

In a large bowl, microwave butter or margarine 35 to 45 seconds on HIGH power or until melted.

Add marshmallows; microwave 1 minute on 70% power. Stir in crisp rice cereal until evenly coated.

Press into a buttered 13'' x 9'' baking dish. Cool and cut into squares.

Makes 24 to 30 squares.

BROWNIES

- 1/2 cup butter or margarine
- 1 cup sugar
- 2 eggs
- 1 teaspoon vanilla extract
- 1/2 cup unsweetened cocoa
- 1/2 cup all-purpose flour

Blend butter or margarine and sugar. Add eggs and vanilla. Beat well. Add dry ingredients. Pour into a greased and sugared round glass cake pan. Microwave 4-1/2 to 5 minutes on HIGH power or 8 to 9 minutes on 50% power.

Makes 15 to 20 brownies.

2-MINUTE FUDGE

- 1 (1-lb.) box powdered sugar
- 1/2 cup unsweetened cocoa
- 1/4 teaspoon salt
- 1/4 cup minus 1 teaspoon milk
- 1 tablespoon vanilla
- 1/2 cup butter or margarine

In a 1-1/2-quart casserole, stir together sugar, cocoa, salt, milk and vanilla until partially blended. Put butter or margarine over top in center of dish. Microwave on HIGH power 2 minutes. Stir well until smooth. Pour into a greased 8-inch square dish. Chill about 1 hour.

Makes about 36 squares.

NUTS AND BOLTS

"Snacks can be fun and nutritious too!"

- 3 cups toasted oat cereal
- 2 cups bite-size wheat cereal squares
- 2 cups thin pretzel sticks
- 1/2 pound mixed nuts
- 1 tablespoon Worcestershire sauce
- 1/2 cup cooking oil
- 2 teaspoons garlic salt
- 2 teaspoons seasoned salt
- 2 dashes Tabasco sauce

Mix all ingredients in a 3-quart casserole dish. Microwave on HIGH power 8 to 10 minutes or until cereal is hot and crisp. Stir twice during cooking. Cool. Keep in an airtight container. Store in a cool place or freeze.

Makes about 10 cups.

CUPCAKE CONES

- 1 (8-oz.) box cake mix
- 8 to 10 flat-bottom ice-cream cones

Prepare cake mix as directed on package. Place 2 tablespoons cake batter in each ice-cream cone. Microwave on HIGH power according to cooking chart below. When you cook more than 2 cupcakes at a time, arrange cupcake cones in a circle in microwave.
Makes 8 cupcake cones.

```
1 —————— 30 to 45 seconds
2 —————— 45 seconds
3 —————— 1 to 1-1/4 minutes
4 —————— 1-1/4 to 1-1/2 minutes
5 —————— 1-3/4 to 2 minutes
6 —————— 2-1/4 to 2-1/2 minutes
7 —————— 2-3/4 to 3 minutes
8 —————— 3-1/4 to 3-1/2 minutes
```

Frost with your favorite frosting.

PINEAPPLE UPSIDE-DOWN CAKE

- 3 tablespoons butter or margarine
- 1/2 cup brown sugar
- 4 slices drained pineapple
- 4 maraschino cherries
- 1 layer yellow or white cake mix or 1/2 of a regular-size cake mix (1-3/4 cups)

Place butter or margarine in a round 8- or 9-inch glass dish. Microwave on HIGH power 35 seconds. Sprinkle brown sugar over butter or margarine.

Arrange pineapple slices in bottom of dish. Place cherries in middle of pineapple slices; set aside.

Prepare cake mix according to package directions using pineapple juice as part of the liquid required. Spread cake batter over pineapple slices, brown sugar and cherries which have been arranged in glass dish.

Microwave on 50% power 5 minutes. Turn. Microwave 2 to 3 minutes on HIGH power. Let stand 5 minutes. Turn cake out onto a serving plate.

Serves 5 to 6.

EASY ORANGE BUNDT CAKE

- 1/4 cup butter or margarine
- 3/4 cup orange marmalade
- 1/2 cup flaked coconut
- 1 package lemon cake mix with pudding
- 3 eggs
- 1/3 cup oil
- 1 cup water

Melt butter or margarine in a 2-cup glass measure 30 seconds on HIGH power. Add marmalade and coconut. Stir to blend. Grease and sugar microwave bundt-cake pan. Spread marmalade mixture on bottom of cake pan. Combine cake mix, eggs, oil and water. Mix well. Pour batter on top of marmalade mixture. Microwave 9 minutes on 50% power and 6-1/2 minutes on HIGH power. Allow to stand 8 minutes before turning cake onto serving platter.

Serves 8 to 10.

ROCKY ROAD CHOCOLATE PIE

- 1 Crumb Pie Crust, see below
- 1 (3-1/2-oz.) box chocolate pudding, not instant
- 2 cups milk
- 1 cup miniature marshmallows
- 1/2 cup chopped walnuts

Mix pudding with milk in a 4-cup glass measure. Microwave on HIGH power 5 to 6 minutes, stirring every 2 minutes or until pudding comes to a boil. Cool. Fold in marshmallows and nuts. Pour into pie shell. Chill. Top with whipped cream if desired.
Serves 6 to 8.

CRUMB PIE CRUST

- 1/3 cup butter or margarine
- 1-1/2 cups cookie crumbs (vanilla wafer, graham cracker or chocolate wafer)
- 3 tablespoons sugar

Place butter or margarine in a glass pie dish. Microwave on 70% power 30 to 45 seconds or until melted. Stir in cookie crumbs and sugar until well blended. Press crumb mixture against bottom and sides of dish. Microwave 2 minutes or until heated through on HIGH power.

ROCKY ROAD
CANDY

- 1 (12-oz.) package semisweet chocolate pieces
- 1 (12-oz.) package butterscotch pieces
- 1 cup peanut butter
- 1 (10-1/2-oz.) package miniature marshamallows
- 1 cup salted peanuts

Combine chocolate and butterscotch pieces with peanut butter in a 2-quart glass measure. Microwave on 70% power 4 to 5 minutes. Stir until melted. Add marshmallows and peanuts. Stir until marshmallows and peanuts are well coated. Spread in a buttered 13" x 9" pan. Refrigerate and cut into squares. For a smaller amount, make half the recipe. Reduce microwave time by half and use an 8-inch square pan.

ABOUT THE AUTHORS

JANET EMAL

As a free-lance home economist, Janet has had the opportunity to write restaurant menus, appear on local radio and TV talk shows, direct and operate day-care centers, and teach microwave cooking classes. She received her B.A. degree in Home Economics from Sacramento State University in California. She is currently teaching at a community college and continues to set up microwave classes in department stores and for private groups. Her background with day-care children and knowledge of microwave cooking combines beautifully for KIDS COOK MICROWAVE!

BARBARA KERN

Barbara received her vocational Home Economics degree from Kansas State University, Manhattan, Kansas. She spent five years teaching home economics in the Wichita Public Schools and now is an energy consultant for an Arizona utility. Her extensive experience with microwave cooking and working with children for the past several years has lead to her interest in KIDS COOK MICROWAVE.

ENDINGS

HAPPY MICROWAVING

NOTES

_____

_____

_____

_____

_____

_____

_____

_____

_____

_____